DOG BLESS AMERICA

Tails from the Road
by Jeff Selis

OLD NAVY

This edition published in 2006 by Chronicle Books LLC exclusively for Old Navy.

The Library of Congress has cataloged the previous edition (ISBN 0-8118-2830-1). Cataloging-in-Publication Data available.

ISBN 10: 0-8118-5543-0
ISBN 13: 978-0-8118-5543-3

Designed by E. Hawthorne Hunt

Manufactured in Singapore

Chronicle Books LLC
85 Second Street
San Francisco, CA 94105

www.chroniclebooks.com
www.oldnavy.com

For Alice and Sam

"Otie!"

Making this book has changed my life forever. The idea came to me at a low point. My mother had recently passed away and I was very "burned out" at work. I knew I needed something fresh in my life—something that would at least let me escape for a while.

My idea was to travel the entire country and meet and photograph at least one dog from every state. I would spend a little time getting to know the dogs, then write about their stories. I wanted to do this because I think dogs are such an important and necessary part of our culture, and they have so much to teach us. In honor of their contribution to our society, I would call it *Dog Bless America.* So I put a proposal together and sent it off to Chronicle Books. To my surprise and delight, they bit.

So, armed with my 1965 Polaroid Land Camera, I hit the road. Riding shotgun was my dear friend Seamus, and panting gleefully in my rearview mirror was my faithful dog, Otis. I'm sure they would tell you that from the first stop to the last, this trip was simply an amazing, surreal and serendipitous experience. It was as if every moment was guided by another force—and we were simply on cruise control. It turned out to be a journey of a lifetime. Not only had I escaped, I had evolved.

On the next page is a map indicating my route around the country. Although the book is in alphabetical order by states, I wanted to include this map so you, the reader, could sense the chronology of the trip. The journey began and ended in my hometown of Portland, Oregon. Walla Walla, Washington, was my first stop and Anchorage, Alaska, was my last. I kept journals of our travels and e-mailed them to my friends and family as I went along. Throughout this book you will find excerpts from those e-mails. I would have liked to share more of my journals, but there simply wasn't enough room for all the words it takes to describe a trek around America. Instead, the following pages are filled with awesome dogs. It is my hope that by the end of this book you will be inspired to love a dog just a little bit more, or perhaps to do something that will make you happier in your own life.

It's so easy to lose perspective in this world. By taking this trip, Seamus and I were able to gain much of ours back. I think we are both greatly indebted to Otis for that. For a while we thought that Otis was becoming more and more like us. But after driving nearly 17,000 miles as a trio, we discovered that the opposite was true; we had become much more like him. We realized that life should be as simple and as pure as a dog's. More importantly, we realized that dogs have not been deprogrammed to stop pursuing what they love. Granted, in Otis's case it's his ball, but he'd go through a wall to find it.

And that's what it's all about.

So I'd just like to say thanks to Otis. Thank you for helping me find my ball.

– Jeff

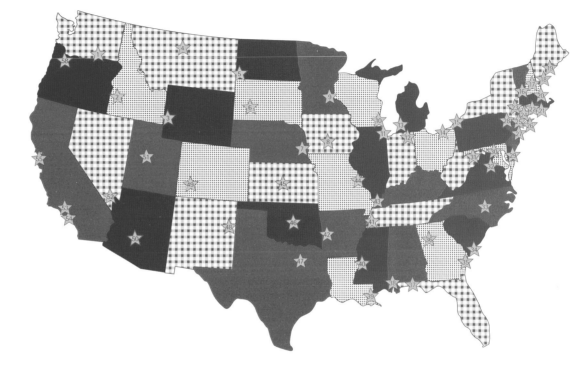

1 Walla Walla, Washington
2 Boise, Idaho
3 Jackson Hole, Wyoming
4 Fort Benton, Montana
5 Marmarth, North Dakota
6 Badlands, South Dakota
7 Omaha, Nebraska
8 Booneville, Iowa
9 St. Paul, Minnesota
10 Kenosha, Wisconsin
11 Chicago, Illinois
12 Mishawaka, Indiana

13 Paw Paw, Michigan
14 Cleveland, Ohio
15 Erie, Pennsylvania
16 Manchester, Vermont
17 Concord, New Hampshire
18 Bath, Maine
19 Warren, Maine
20 Cambridge, Massachusetts
21 Newport, Rhode Island
22 Greenwich, Connecticut
23 North Salem, New York
24 Golden's Bridge, New York

25 Hastings on Hudson, New York
26 New York, New York
27 Jersey City, New Jersey
28 Morristown, New Jersey
29 Newark, Delaware
30 Libertytown, Maryland
31 Sheperdstown, West Virginia
32 Arlington, Virginia
33 Tar Heel, North Carolina
34 Hilton Head, South Carolina
35 Savannah, Georgia
36 Atlanta, Georgia

37 Pensacola Beach, Florida
38 Mobile, Alabama
39 New Orleans, Louisiana
40 Vicksburg, Mississippi
41 Memphis, Tennessee
42 Mount Ida, Arkansas
43 Paducah, Kentucky
44 St. Louis, Missouri
45 Rome, Kansas
46 Oklahoma City, Oklahoma
47 Dallas, Texas
48 Tucumcari, New Mexico

49 Durango, Colorado
50 Phoenix, Arizona
51 Angel Canyon, Utah
52 Las Vegas, Nevada
53 Hollywood, California
54 Los Angeles, California
55 San Francisco, California
56 Honolulu, Hawaii
57 Anchorage, Alaska
58 Portland, Oregon

5

Greetings from Alabama!

Once we're all loaded up and on the road, it's a sight to behold. The van is jammed full of stuff. We have dozens of bags, mostly full of way too many clothes; a year's supply of dog food for a three month trip; tennis balls and chewed up Frisbees; camera gear and loads of film; tons of maps; empty coolers; a power generator for our cell phone, computer and CD player; and personalized mugs we received as gifts from my brother Sam that read "Maverick" and "Goose."

★★★★★★★★★★★★★★★★★★★★★★★★★★★★★★★★

Shorty

Sounds like Shorty got the short end of the stick in the looks department. According to his mom, he's got a face only a mother could love.

Shorty's not too worried about his looks though. Rest assured that whatever he lacks in appearance, he more than makes up for in personality.

7

Aztec, Bob Jones, Cecil, F-150, 4-runner, Frasier, Horst, Inca, McQueen, Ol'Spice, Ranger and Stealth

Known as fifty-pound dogs with one hundred-pound hearts, these twelve pups live to race. And all are veterans of the biggest race known to dog: the Iditarod.

The Iditarod covers a mere 1100 miles over just about every terrain imaginable— be it steep snowy mountains, frozen tundra, open water or gravel. And let's not forget about the elements—the freezing rain, the driving snow, the bitter cold or, horror of horrors, above freezing temperatures!

These dogs trek up to 150 miles in a 24-hour period and burn nearly 11,000 calories in the same timeframe. 11,000 calories! As far as their three-time champion musher is concerned, his dogs are the most incredible athletes in the world—on four legs OR two.

Henry

A dog of means, by no means, Henry's king of the road. He spends most of his days riding shotgun in his momma's eighteen-wheeler. The only state he hasn't been to is the one that doesn't have a road to it—Hawaii. But that doesn't mean he's against hopping on a plane some-day for a vacation.

Henry loves meeting new people, is very friendly and will even talk to you. What he will tell you is that he loves apples, wrestling, running and watching the miles roll by while his ears flap free in the wind.

Grover Cleveland

Grover Cleveland wanted to see what the big deal was with Mt. Rushmore, so he and his family made the long drive across the country to check it out.

Grover was impressed with the carved heads of his fellow former presidents, but figured he was better off immortalized as a dog.

He did manage to mark some of his own territory near the monument before making his way back home.

Sir Harry of Hollywood

Sir Harry of Hollywood has never
been in a movie, nor has he ever been
on TV. The one time he had the
opportunity to be in a commercial he
slept in instead.

No, fame is not his game. The only
attention Harry needs is from his
master, the same guy who plucked
him out of the parking lot of the
7–Eleven where he'd been abandoned.

Harry loves riding in the car, sleeping
on the heater, and running like the
wind at the park. With perks like these,
who needs fame?

B'wana

According to B'wana's mom, he stood in line twice for beauty but not once for brains.

He's smart enough to know what he wants out of life though, and that's his daily trip to Alamo Square Park, right across the street from San Francisco's famous "Painted Ladies."

As for heart, B'wana's got a lot of it, and he hopes to never have to leave it in San Francisco.

Carter

Carter was named after the famous magician Carter the Great. While he doesn't know as many magic tricks as his namesake, he can make a bowl of dog food disappear like nobody's business.

One thing he couldn't make disappear was the skunk smell that mysteriously enveloped him after one of his daily sniffing expeditions. Carter the Great had become Carter the Stinky.

It was only after much time had passed, and many spells were cast, that this Carter was Great once again.

15

Greetings from Colorado!

I'm not entirely sure what Otis thinks of his new life out here on the road, but I think he thinks it's pretty cool. He's definitely become accustomed to the routine of it. It's so funny because every morning when we wake up, no matter where we are, his first instinct after doing his business is to hop in the car and wait patiently for departure. It's like he knows we're on a journey. He's enjoying each experience as its own but he knows not to get used to it. And once we hit the road, he places his two front paws on the front seat armrests and assumes his lookout position in between Seamus and me. Once he's satisfied that we're headed for unmarked territory, he retires to the back for some more sleep, knowing full well that when he wakes up he will find a treasure of new smells.

★ ★

One Ton

One Ton is so tall he has a different lifestyle than most other dogs. For example, if he's thirsty he doesn't just drink water from a bowl. Instead he goes to the refrigerator and dispenses ice from the icemaker with his nose.

He has also taught himself to play the piano, thanks to his exceptionally long legs. Word has it he's tone deaf, but it's all sweet music to One Ton's ears.

Duster

Duster got his name because of his resemblance to a feather duster. This should by no means imply that Duster is into cleaning house. He'd much prefer to spend his time getting dirty in the yard with Camelot, his wife of the same breed.

Duster won Camelot over with his soulful black eyes and his gentlemanly ways. He affectionately awakens his wife every morning and always lets her go through the door first.

Duster is seventy-seven years old going on seven. His wife wonders when he'll ever slow down. One thing that will always stop him in his tracks is a "tummy tickle."

Shaggy

Shaggy is a product of our nation's first state. His owners found him wandering down one of its roads.

Shaggy loves kids, especially his big sister who dotes on him daily. He's also feline friendly. Just ask Tippy, his favorite cat.

Shaggy detests collars and leashes, which might explain his nomadic origins.

Buck

Buck lives on what are claimed to
be "the whitest beaches in the
world." Unfortunately for Buck, the
beaches aren't dog friendly. Of
course, this doesn't stop him from
sneaking off to jump in the surf
every chance he gets.

Every time Buck heads for the sand
he risks being arrested, but ask him
and he'll tell you that a night in
the slammer is more than worth it
for a day at the beach.

You dig?

We woke up rested and made our way to Krispy Kreme—home of America's favorite donuts. If there's one thing that really jumps out at you in the South, it's Krispy Kreme donuts. Truthfully, I think that Krispy Kreme has some weird "force field" that won't allow you to drive by without some serious contemplation of stopping, no matter what time of day it is. Seamus can't stand how good these donuts are. As for me, I had never had one until this trip and never believed all of Seamus's hype. Now, it's all I can do to just keep driving.

Speaking of driving, we're moving along with purpose, conquering the South just like General Grant and General Sherman back in the day. We're not lighting any fires, but we're definitely leaving our mark.

★ ★

Max

If Max were a character in the book *Midnight in the Garden of Good and Evil*, he would only represent the good part.

His favorite time of the day is when he and his buddies get together at Colonial Cemetery—the oldest cemetery in Savannah. As it's no longer an active cemetery, it's been designated as a dog park and is the only place in town where dogs can socialize off-leash.

And speaking of socializing, Max has mingled with dogs from all over the world. He's traveled to Mexico, China, Japan, England and Germany. He even understands some German.

Guten dog, Max. Guten Dog.

23

Gemini

Gemini: May 21–June 20

Your unique duality offers you twice
as much stimulation as other dogs.
Trees are your power objects. Your
cycle is high. Your bowl is always
half full, never half empty. Treats
are forever in your future.

Pahu

Pahu is a Poi dog, which means "mixed breed" in the Hawaiian language. Poi is also a form of food, which makes sense because Pahu's favorite thing to do is eat. She dines regularly on sushi and sashimi, but her favorite meal is artichokes and Chardonnay.

The name Pahu means "Hawaiian drum," which is a popular percussion instrument heard around the Island. She was given the name after being drawn to its sound. Pahu is also drawn to the rhythm of the waves along the beaches of Hawaii.

Pahu's favorite word is "aloha," but only when it means "hello."

Kashmir and Chibi

Kashmir has Attention Deficit Disorder and Chibi has a low thyroid. Other than that, these two have got it made.

They spend their days playing chase in the yard, and their nights dining on pasta with red sauce.

They've both been bitten by the travel bug. Their owners indulge their hunger for the open road a lot more now that Kashmir and Chibi know to keep quiet while being sneaked past motel clerks who are suspicious of panting, oddly lumpy gym bags.

    Well, it's off to conquer Chicago. Look for us on *SportsCenter*. I'm planning on parking Otis outside the leftfield wall of Wrigley Field with hopes that he'll fetch Sammy Sosa's next dinger. Hey, you never know.

"30"

When asked what "30" would consider his most heroic feat, one of his firemen replied, "Catching a rat."

"30" is always the first one on the truck, but he doesn't get too involved with the actual fire fighting anymore. He learned early on that being carried out of a burning building is not quite as fun as running into one.

Still, "30" is a hero to all the men he represents at Engine 30—the second oldest firehouse in the city of Chicago.

At least they don't have to worry about rats.

Abby

Zen and the Art of Quail Hunting is
what it's all about for Abby. Her
best days are when her master takes
her out on the farm for a game of
hide and go seek the quail.

Just a pup, Abby is still mastering
her technique, but ask any of the
disgruntled quails and they'll tell
you she's doing just fine.

Not to worry, Abby is very gentle
when she discovers them. She
seems to understand that they are
an integral part of the game so
she's careful not to wound them.
She prefers to sink her teeth into
cardboard.

Greetings from Iowa!

I think the most satisfying aspect our journey thus far has been meeting the couples we've encountered along the way. It seems that the one constant everywhere we've gone is a working relationship—two people who love and respect each other and know the other inside and out. Alice and I are only in our second year of marriage, but meeting these couples on the road, I've witnessed firsthand what commitment means. What I want more than anything in this life is a long, healthy relationship with my partner. It is clear to me that it's the most important part of life.

Danny

Danny is as corn-fed as they come. When he's not eating corn he likes to pretend he's a frog by eating bugs. When he's not eating bugs he's probably busy chewing up someone's shoes.

But what Danny loves to do most is ride in the car with his family. In his mind, it's the only thing that makes up for being banished to the garage for snacking on dad's favorite boots.

KANSAS

Maggie

When in Rome, do as Maggie. There aren't more than thirty people in the whole town, but that never keeps Maggie from finding a good time.

The only thing that can dampen her spirits is the dreaded tornado. If there's one thing she never wants to hear, it's that she's not in Kansas anymore.

Nope, there's no place like home.

34

Wags

If it were up to Wags, he would break bread everyday. It's his favorite thing to eat.

One time Wags's owner noticed he wasn't eating his regular food. Then he realized that there was an entire loaf of bread missing from the kitchen table. Turns out Wags had stashed it in his bed and was bringing it into the TV room, slice by slice.

TV dinner took on a whole new meaning.

Greetings from Louisiana!

We spent the last two days introducing Seamus to the finer points of living. We weren't in New Orleans for more than five minutes before Seamus had assumed the entire city as his soul mate. The three of us couldn't get enough of Bourbon Street. It was the first time all trip that Otis was ready for bed before we were. He hit the wall at 1 A.M. We begrudgingly took him back to our Motel 6.

Oil

Oil is easily the most popular dog in the French Quarter. He's even mentioned in the *Frommer's Guide to New Orleans*. Take a sightseeing carriage ride through the Quarter and you will more than likely hear your escort mention him by name.

Speaking of his name, it's pronounced "Earl"—as in, "Have you change'd the earl in the car lately?" We're talking down-the-bayou, Cajun-style accents here.

"Earl" loves attention. He even went so far as to dress up as a drag queen for his first Mardi Gras.

Laissez les bon temps rouler, Oil. Let the good times roll.

WARREN
MAINE

V Iso Vom Forskamp SchH III

Call him Iso. Stud Iso.

Iso was imported from Germany in the fall of 1998. Since then he has studded a great number of puppies. Iso's offspring have found homes all across the country. Some are family companions, some are guard dogs and some are police service dogs. All, Iso would have you know, have inherited his wonderful personality.

Iso loves nothing more than a rendezvous with the girls, but in his down time he's pretty content just knowing he's THE DOG.

Lola

Most dogs would be intimidated by the thought of living in a place called Bath, but Lola fears nothing.

Squirrels live in fear of her, though, as she is a Lakeland Terrier by breed and loves a good chase.

She is indifferent to other dogs unless they are stuffed. Lola can't get enough of her stuffed animals.

Sir Winston Churchill the 28th

On June 18, 1940, Prime Minister Winston Churchill declared: "Hitler knows that he will have to break us in this island or lose the war. If we can stand up to him, all Europe may be free and the life of the world may move forward into broad, sunlit uplands. But if we fail, then the whole world, including the United States, including all that we have known and cared for, will sink into the abyss of a new dark age, made more sinister and perhaps more protracted, by the light of perverted science. Let us therefore brace ourselves to our duties, and so bear ourselves that, if the British Empire and its Commonwealth last for a thousand years, men will say, 'This was their finest hour.'"

With all due respect to his namesake, Sir Winston Churchill the 28th considers his finest hour the one when he's chasing the little red dot that projects from his owner's cool laser pointer.

To each his own.

Jackpot Jr. a.k.a. Potsky

Ten reasons it's better to be "Potsky" than human:

1. Hair products produce tangible results.
2. More intelligent.
3. Less willing to bite when provoked.
4. Better looking.
5. Halitosis is more susceptible to treatment.
6. Less vain.
7. Good table manners.
8. Looks good without clothes.
9. Acts appropriately in public.
10. Can be taught things.

List compiled by "Potsky's" human.

Cody

Cody makes her home on Paw Paw Road in Paw Paw, Michigan.

Her favorite thing to get her own paws on is a rock. Forget bones or balls or Frisbees, she's not interested. But she'll fetch a rock all day long.

The good news for her parents is that it saves money on toys at the pet store. The bad news is, one bad throw and it's hello tooth doctor.

Franklin

Call him the First Dog of Minnesota. Franklin is the loyal pet of Governor Jesse "The Body" Ventura.

Loyal as he may be to the Guv and First Lady, he loves company to the extent that he will lie on your feet to keep you from leaving.

Franklin never misses a photo-op, and he's bipartisan on everything but chipmunks. That's where this politician draws the party line.

MISSISSIPPI

Roxie

Roxie makes her home in the historic town of Vicksburg, Mississippi, the site of one of the bloodiest battles of the Civil War. According to President Lincoln, the Battle of Vicksburg was "the key" to ending the battle between North and South.

While history doesn't much interest Roxie, she knows, sadly enough, what it's like to be shot. At the time this photo was taken she was nursing a gunshot wound received from a disgruntled neighbor.

History or no history, Roxie knows one thing all too well—War is Hell.

Mr. Jeffries

Mr. Jeffries was a rare find. He is a purebred Standard Poodle who was dropped at the local Humane Society simply for having a little too much pep in his step.

Maybe that's why Mr. Jeffries's favorite time of the year is when the city holds its annual Woofstock festival. He loves marching in the parade and dressing up for the costume contest. This year's costume garnered him the runner-up trophy. (He lost out to a Scooby Doo look-alike!)

If living life to its fullest were considered a contest, Mr. Jeffries would win every time.

Riley

Riley represents "the gateway to the West"—St. Louis, Missouri.

Riley was born in three feet of snow and to this day can't seem to get enough of it. During the warmer months he loves swimming and chasing squirrels. The boys of summer don't interest him much, but that doesn't mean he'd be opposed to fetching a Mark McGwire homer some day.

I find I'm using a lot of swear words as I discover the beauty of it all.

We arrived in Fort Benton, Montana, on Friday afternoon and immediately found the statue of Old Shep. Otis hopped out of the car and went straight over to give the old dog a sniff. Not as impressed as the thousands who come through the historic town to see the dog, Otis jumped down and started marking Shep's territory instead.

We were soon befriended by the town's fourteen-year-old juvenile delinquent. He told us he'd just finished his twenty hours of community service that he had to serve for missing his curfew. He hung out with us for the better part of the afternoon and took us up to Old Shep's burial site. Before we dropped him off, he pointed out the Sunrise Bluff Retirement Home where he said we would find old Kenny Vinion. Kenny played "Taps" at Shep's funeral in 1942. When we asked Kenny if he still played the horn he replied, "not since I lost all my teeth."

Shep

As the legend goes, Shep's master—a local sheepherder—passed away back in 1936. His casket was placed on a train headed East for burial. Shep followed the casket to the train station and anxiously watched as it disappeared in the distance. Certain his master would return, Shep remained at the side of the tracks. He waited and waited. He checked every train that came in. He checked them for five years. His master never returned.

One day Shep slipped on the icy tracks in front of an incoming train and died. His vigil had come to an end. Hundreds of people attended his funeral. A Boy Scout played "Taps." The entire town mourned.

It was a sad time in the storied history of Fort Benton, but perhaps the locals found solace knowing Shep had finally reunited with his master.

Eve of Destruction

With a name befitting of the Nebraska Cornhuskers football team, Eve of Destruction does all of her damage off the gridiron. She got her name because of all that she destroyed when she came home as a young pup.

Not one for accepting penalties, she has conformed to playing by house rules, and goes simply by "Eve" now.

Kelly

Kelly is a highly regarded tracker, and if you know anything about tracking, you'll know she's earning a reputation as one of the best. Tracking is a skills test among dogs who use scent and speed to find a planted glove. Kelly's so good they probably could have called her as an expert witness in a long and painful trial not so long ago.

Knowing Kelly, she probably would have pleaded the fifth and headed out for a swim.

Tahoe

An Ivy Leaguer, Tahoe spent his early days roaming the college campus at Dartmouth. He and his four-legged fraternity brothers gave bona fide meaning to the term "Animal House."

A little too much partying turned into a wild night with some sorority cats and he wound up in the doghouse. After being placed on double secret probation he was unable to make the grade and eventually sent home to Concord.

Wild days behind him, he's now on the household honor roll.

Lucky

It's better to be Lucky than good.

Regal

Ever tried to keep up with a blind woman and her dog on their way to pick up their morning coffee? It's impossible!

Regal loves life. What she loves most is working. She loves leading her proud owner to and from work every day along the streets of Morristown, New Jersey. And how many dogs can say they get to spend every waking moment with their human?

By trade, Regal is a courageous dog, but when the thunderstorms roll in she's the one who needs assistance.

Babe

Would you get hip to this kindly tip
And go take that California trip...

Babe gets her kicks on Route 66. Her favorite hobby is riding
in her dad's truck. She does most of her cruising along Route
66 in Tucumcari, New Mexico, but her real ambition is to cover
every single mile of the 2,448.

...Well it winds from Chicago to L.A.
More than 2000 miles all the way
Get your kicks on Route 66.

Well, the epiphany has happened. I half expected that it would sometime along this trip. And it did today. At the Cathedral Church of Saint John the Divine during the Feast of Saint Francis—an annual "party" to which all creation is invited, including the animals. Much like many of the people we've met on our journey, Saint Francis was a man of profound hospitality and broad welcoming spirit, and it is because of these fundamental qualities he is celebrated as this party's host. As with the good timing of most of our trip, this celebration fell on the weekend we just so happened to be passing through.

At one point the man spoke of Jesus Christ. He said Jesus was born and his mission was one of love. He wanted to gather people. He wanted everyone to get along. He wanted to give love and be loved. As I listened to these words I looked around for Otis. I couldn't see him. I looked behind me and there he was, on the lap of this total stranger—a man legally blind, and Otis was licking him all over his face. Here was the epiphany. The celebration of the animals. The celebration of Otis. Everything the man was saying about Jesus Christ could also be said about Otis. Mind you, please don't think I am taking anything away from Jesus, but you should see this dog of mine. He's a loyal dog, I guess, but he's more interested in making other people happy, making other people smile. He gathers people. They look at him and say, "My, what an interesting dog." He snorts and they laugh. He wags his tail and they pet him. I'm pretty sure I could have walked away from Otis at that moment and he would have continued to find love and happiness and give love and happiness for the rest of his life. I like to think that he would miss me, but I'm pretty sure he would survive. For Otis, like Jesus, it's all about the love.

Muffy

Muffy is a "lady who lunches" and she only dines in the finest of establishments.

According to Muffy's owner she doesn't even realize she's a dog, and judging from her appearance, one wonders if other dogs might be equally confused.

The wonderful upside of her unique appearance is all the extra attention she gets. One time, while she was dining at a Manhattan restaurant, a line of people formed all the way around the corner just to sneak a peak.

Of course, being a true "lady who lunches," Muffy remained quite blasé about the entire affair.

NORTH SALEM
NEW YORK

Fanny

Fanny spends her time vying for attention from her six-year-old brother, David. Pokémon is her competition by day, but when the lights go out David is all hers.

She keeps a lookout from the foot of his bed every night and protects him from all those imaginary monsters.

Fanny is also a pleaser, but given the choice between pleasing or chewing up a down pillow, she'll choose the down pillow every time.

Scout, Crystal, Major, Bashful, Laughter, Ziggy, Zelda, Linda, Visit, Vixen, Andy, Beckett, Helper, Lucy, Yuri, Cautious, Uncle, Merlin, Jo-Jo, Justice, Nectar, Rebel, Busy, Banker, Governor, Pilot, Judy, Josie, Murphy, Bill, Boom, Battle, Ned and Noah

Known as the Pennmarydel Golden's Bridge Hounds, this pack is more fearsome than the one in Green Bay.

Just ask Mister Fox. He's the one running for his life come the weekend hunt.

Taco

Taco is mellow and undaunted. How else could you describe someone who has no qualms about sunning himself in bustling Times Square?

However, Taco very much dislikes and resents the talking Chihuahua he keeps seeing on TV, so much so that he demanded his name be changed to "Choo-Choo" until the ad campaign is pulled.

Isn't our world amazing? It's full of poop and shootings and hurricanes, but it's also full of amazing people who will answer the phone and open their doors and put food on the table and provide a comfortable bed and a warm shower and a place to simply catch your breath. Time and time again on this trip it has happened for us. And that's pretty cool.

Candy

Q: Why did the chicken cross the road?

A: Probably because Candy chased her.

Candy's favorite activity is hounding the chickens that roam the grounds of her home in Tar Heel, North Carolina. Much to her dismay, it's Candy who usually gets cooped up.

67

NORTH DAKOTA

Spook

Spook got her name because she came home on Halloween. That was sixteen years ago, which in dog years is 112 years ago. Now that's scary!

It's also fitting that she would start her life with her family on Halloween because she's so sweet. Like candy.

Big Dawg

Big Dawg is the founder of the Cleveland Browns' "Dawg Pound," a pack of fanatics who pledge their allegiance on any given Sunday.

When he was abandoned by an owner who moved the Browns to another city a few years back, Big Dawg waited patiently for a new owner to bring the team home again.

His patience was rewarded. Big Dawg again dreams of barking his team all the way to the Super Bowl. But one senses that even if the team never won another game it wouldn't really matter to Big Dawg.

That's because he's as loyal as they come.

Ranger

Don't try doing anything illegal in Oklahoma. If you do, chances are Ranger will catch you.

With over sixty narcotics apprehensions and hundreds of pounds of drugs recovered, Ranger is well on his way to being one of Oklahoma's most decorated K-9 dogs. In addition to his narcotics prowess, he has fourteen tracking apprehensions so far, including a homicide suspect who had shot a police officer.

Ranger has also busted six burglary suspects and has recovered several thousand of dollars worth of U.S. currency.

Consider yourself warned.

Otis

When the question "Go for a ride?" means a trip to the nearest grocery store, Otis will burst with joy. So imagine how excited he was when his daddy—the author of this book—opened the car door and invited him along for a little jaunt around the country. Otis had hit the motherlode.

Otis's portion of the journey covered 17,000 miles, enabled him to mark territory in each of the continental forty-eight and provided him glorious new smells all along the way—mostly of the four-legged variety.

Unfortunately for Otis, his travels came to an end. Back to the daily grind of eating and sleeping, Otis waits anxiously for his next ticket to ride.

Czar

Czar lives in a world of coincidence.

His favorite activity is playing in the water... he now lives on Lake Erie— the biggest lake in the world. His birth name was Czar... he was later adopted by a Russian immigrant.

It would take the powers of Rasputin to divine the significance of this fated pup.

Marty

Marty will eat anything from A to Z. That's Apples to Zucchini. Be careful though, because he doesn't like people around him when he's eating. So don't even think about asking him to pass the peas.

Marty is getting up there in years and is now partially blind. He's deaf too, but only when he wants to be.

Travelin' Bodey

Travelin' Bodey got his name for the miles he's put on while touring the country with his owner.

His summer months are spent on the shores of Hilton Head Island helping his master with his Wave Runner business. Bodey does his part by showing people how easy it is to take a ride. He will do anything if it involves playing in water.

Bodey's favorite thing to do is swim. His one aspiration is to learn to swim underwater. That way, he could fetch up those rocks that keep sinking to the bottom.

As the place filled up with the regulars, a couple of Native Americans showed up and Mayor Reichardt had to excuse himself to go barter with them. The mayor didn't give 'em much business so they came over to see what they could sell to me and Seamus.

"We need ten dollars for gas money to make it home. Buy this tent," the wife pressed.

"I don't need a tent," I replied, "how 'bout I buy you a beer instead?"

"And some chips," she added.

I bought her pretzels but she couldn't eat them because just like old Kenny Vinion, she didn't have any teeth.

"No teeth. Need chips," she demanded.

"You go pick them out," I said.

We chatted with them over a beer before giving them ten bucks and going on our way. The husband looked me dead in the eye and said, "You are a good soul. I will remember you."

"Thank you," I said, as the toothless wife gave me a big, strong hug.

Bones

Bones is one of the best hunters you'll ever find who doesn't carry a gun.

His job is to track down coyotes that prey on the area livestock. Bones is not your ordinary house pet, but he's as devoted as they come. His master claims that he would risk tail and limb in his effort to catch the wily coyote.

Rock and Roll

The King is gone but he's not forgotten.

Rock and Roll pay tribute to him every day just by having their names called for dinner. Rock plays the part of Fat Elvis while Roll clings to the guise of Skinny Elvis.

Even the King would agree that these two ain't just a couple of hound dogs.

Kate

Kate is a purebred Bloodhound who used to work with Sierra Madre Search and Rescue. She once picked up a twenty-nine-hour-old scent of a child who was lost in the Sierra Madre Mountain Range. Shortly thereafter, the child was found and brought home safely.

Long since retired, Kate now uses her trusty nose to sniff out her favorite discovery: food.

Muffin

Muffin was found on the side of the freeway when he was three months old. The people who found him were members of Best Friends Animal Sanctuary, which is the largest no-kill animal shelter in the country.

Muffin is now four years old and greets visitors in the welcome center every day of the week. Best Friends places more than 75 percent of the 1800 animals they house every year. For those that never find a new home their consolation is living out the rest of their lives in one of the most beautiful and peaceful places in the entire U.S., and all with unwavering commitment and care.

It's a must visit if you're ever in the neighborhood. And just so you know, Muffin loves belly rubs.

Greetings from Vermont!

We stayed with the parents of a college roommate of Seamus's in Manchester. This place was unbelievable. Had my wife been there with me, I'm pretty sure she would have had our home in Portland on the market by now. We stayed for two nights and took it all in—the trees, the sky, the sunset and the stars. I'm telling you I've never seen so many stars. And their backyard was a polo field that used to be a grass airstrip, a field that once belonged to Robert Todd Lincoln—son of Abe. Thankfully for Otis, there were no polo matches going on, so he had the entire grounds to himself. We headed back to Walt and Nancy's one night (Seamus's friend's parents) and found a note on the counter that read: "Boys, dinner in the oven—beer in the fridge." Walt and Nancy had an engagement at the golf club. I was floored. Remember that line in *Field of Dreams* when the guy says, "Is this heaven?" And Kevin Costner says, "No, it's Iowa." Well, I think he should have said, "No, it's Vermont."

Tillie

Tillie passed away shortly after this photograph was taken. She was eleven years old when she died. During those eleven years her days were filled with back scratches and eating fresh vegetables from the garden.

At the dinner table she would patiently stare down her master until he would finally give in and hand down a scrap. Night after night, it never failed.

Tillie loved being loved. Rainy days and Mondays were the only things that got her down.

ARLINGTON
VIRGINIA

Genrick

Genrick is a purebred Bedlington Terrier.

What he loves to do most is socialize,
whether it's with people, other dogs, or
even cats. He just loves company.

He's a very happy-go-lucky guy. His
friends will tell you that the only thing
that will bother him is a bad hair day.

Daisy

Daisy lives for cows. In fact, she'd rather herd cattle than eat. She's received two broken jaws on the job—the last of which she ignored until her work was done.

Daisy is now twelve years old, and any talk of sending her out to pasture is pure hogwash as far as she is concerned.

WEST VIRGINIA

Sandy

According to Sandy's owners, she's a Labrador/Polar Bear mix. They say she'll eat anything, which is one reason this photographer didn't get too close.

As a polar bear should, Sandy loves playing in the snow on a cold winter's day. It follows that a really hot day tends to slow her down.

Although summer heat won't send her into hibernation, fireworks and thunder sometimes do the trick.

Moo

Moo is known as the most Velcro of
dogs. He sticks to you.

While never favored to win the big
race, he was always a favorite at
the track.

Had Moo ever caught the rabbit he
was chasing he probably would
have just licked it and hoped they
could be friends.

Greetings from Wyoming!

We made our way down to the famous "Cowboy Bar" where we met all sorts of interesting people. Seamus befriended an older cowboy with a worn-out hat and glasses as thick as the bottom of our beer mugs. The guy was drunk as a skunk and had a herd of cowgirls around listening to his stories. Seamus had found his hero.

★★★★★★★★★★★★★★★★★★★★★★★★★★★★★★★★

Loup

Loup—named after his master's hometown of Loup, Nebraska—has got everything a dog could ever hope for. He lives in a cabin on a lake at the base of the Grand Tetons where he's got an endless supply of tennis balls.

Most days are spent chasing the balls his master serves into the middle of the lake. Word has it Loup never lost a match.

Tennis anyone?

93

ACKNOWLEDGMENTS

This book was made possible in part because of major contributions from two of my all-time favorite companies, Motel 6 and the Polaroid Corporation.

To Motel 6, I say thanks for always leaving the light on. The blue sign with the red 6 in the sky

was always such a welcome sight at the end of a long day on the road. And had it not been for your wonderful, pet-friendly policy I wouldn't have been able to travel with my dog, Otis, which is to say that my experience would have never meant as much to me. So I thank you for that.

And speaking of Otis, I know he too would send special thanks if he could. There's nothing he loves more than riding in the car all day, but he also likes a sense of routine. With the consistency in the design and layout of your rooms, I was convinced that after a long, wonderful day of new smells and experiences, Otis thought he was returning to the same place every night. Whether he really thought this or not I can't be sure, but I am sure that he was very content in the comfort of his surroundings. In other words, he doesn't get to sleep on the bed at home!

To Polaroid, I can't thank you enough. Your generous donation of film can only be compared to the time I walked into the candy store as a seven-year-old kid and the guy behind the counter told me I could take as much candy as I wanted. Okay, that didn't really happen, but if it did that's what I would compare it to.

All of the photographs in this book were taken with my 1965 Polaroid Land Camera 180. It's my favorite toy in my box. I can only think of a few things I enjoy more than the instant gratification of a Polaroid picture—especially one with a dog in it. I can't thank everyone at Polaroid enough for supplying me with so much "candy." And the great thing is, I won't even get any cavities!

To my wife and boy, I love you both. I know that the three-month separation was tremendously difficult, but what I've taken away from this journey will benefit us all for a lifetime. Here's to the future journeys we take together.

To my dog, Otis, I'm sorry we passed so many parks along the way, buddy, but I'm so grateful you stuck with me. I learned more from you than from any other aspect of this trip. You are the true definition of love. If only we could all spread it and accept it as well as you.

To my dear friend Seamus, thank you for putting your life on hold and taking this trip with me. Like I've said before, it started as my journey, but it soon became yours, too. I will never forget this experience for as long as I live. Long live Maverick and Goose!

To my employer Wieden & Kennedy, I can't thank you enough. What a rare company in this world, to encourage its employees to find such outlets of creativity and sanity-savers for the betterment of its workers. I can't count how many people actually said to me, "And your company is just letting you go to do this?" Thank you from the bottom of my heart.

To my dear old dad; if you were a dog, your tail would never stop wagging and your tongue would always be out. Thank you, Dad, for never failing to show us kids what life is supposed to be all about.

To my brothers and sisters, thank you for always being there for me.

To my mom, thanks for continuing to be here with me. You were with me every mile of the 17,000.

To Chet, Henry, Ruby and all my future nephews, nieces and children, I hope you wear this book out learning the name of each dog and how to read all about them.

To all my friends, relatives and co-workers I say thank you for taking this ride with me. It may be a small world, but this country can be huge and vast. My e-mails to all of you were my lifeline to home. Thank you so much for writing back.

To Chronicle Books I say thank you for this opportunity. You guys are the best. And, Micaela, thank you so much for taking all my calls, getting me over my blocks, and giving me so much attention. I can only hope that we get to do this again.

To all the folks we met along the way, thank you for the kindness, hospitality and willingness to accept the three of us into your worlds. Either dogs are an unfailing way to gain access to a stranger's trust, or this country is made up of some pretty amazing people. Thank you for feeding us, thank you for boarding us, thank you for taking us sailing and thank you for confirming my belief in the values of commitment and love.

Last but not least, to all the dogs who mark this great land of ours, thank you for letting me into your territory. I hope I've represented you in the way that you deserve.

P.S. Thanks again, Hawthorne. And, of course, your silly cat too.